SELECTED POEMS OF
SEÁN Ó RÍORDÁIN
IN TRANSLATION

Greg Delanty

GREG DELANTY was born in Cork City, Ireland in 1958 and lived in Cork until 1986. Since then he lives most of the year in Vermont where he teaches at St. Michael's College. For three months of each year he returns to his Irish home in Derrynane, County Kerry. He has received numerous awards for his poetry including The Patrick Kavanagh Award (1983), The Allan Dowling Poetry Fellowship (1986), and the Austin Clarke Centenary Poetry Award (1997). In 2007 he was granted a Guggenheim for Poetry. He has received an Irish Arts Council Bursary, and has been widely anthologised. Greg Delanty's seven collections of poems were brought together in his *Collected Poems 1986–2006*, published by The Oxford Poet's Series of Carcanet Press in 2006.

SELECTED POEMS OF
SEÁN Ó RÍORDÁIN
IN TRANSLATION

Greg Delanty

NEW
ISLAND

SELECTED POEMS OF SEÁN Ó RÍORDÁIN IN TRANSLATION

First published 2007
by New Island
2 Brookside
Dundrum Road
Dublin 14
www.newisland.ie

Copyright © Translation into English: Greg Delanty 2007

The right of Greg Delanty to be identified as the Author/Translator of this work has been asserted with the Copyright and Related Rights Act 2000.

ISBN 978-1-905494-44-6

British Library Cataloguing Data. A CIP catalogue record for this book is available from the British Library.

Book design by Inka Hagen
Printed in Ireland by Colour Books Ltd.

New Island received financial assistance from
The Arts Council (An Chomhairle Ealaíon), Dublin, Ireland.

10 9 8 7 6 5 4 3 2 1

Acknowledgements

Agenda, An Leabar Mór – The Great Book of Gaelic, Fulcrum, Literary Imagination, Poetry Ireland Review, Poetry Review.

I wish to show gratitude to Liam Ó Muirthile. These translations would not have been possible without his help. I am grateful to Seán Ó Coileáin and Seán Ó Mórdha – the literary executors of Seán Ó Ríordáin – for their support, advice and blessing. I want to thank Barra Ó Seaghdha and David Curzon for their help with the translations.

I also want to acknowledge Joan O'Riordan, John O'Riordan and the O'Riordan family, the nearest living relatives of Seán Ó Ríordáin, for their written support of this book.

I am grateful to Saint Michael's College, Colchester, Vermont, for a grant that assisted me in completing this project.

Contents

from *Kindling – Brosna* (1964)

from *Limbo Lines – Línte Liombó* (1971)

from *After My Death – Tar Éis mo Bháis* (1978)

Preface

Anthologies of Irish poetry with English-language translations, no matter how fine they are, generally represent Seán Ó Ríordáin with a combination of the same few poems: 'My Mother's Burial', 'Behind the House', 'Exchange', 'Death', 'Claustrophobia', 'Frozen', 'Mount Melleray' and 'The Moths'. All these poems, with the exception of 'Behind the House', are preoccupied with struggle, sorrow, sickness and death. No anthology adequately reflects the range of zest, humour, word-play and subject matter of Ó Ríordáin's corpus. Poems like 'Syllabling' or 'Catology' exude exuberance, as does the darker poem 'Freedom'. 'Tulyar' is one of the funniest satirical critiques of the attitude to sex in mid-twentieth century Catholic Ireland, matching any similar attack by Patrick Kavanagh or Austin Clarke. Indeed, like the work of these two contempories of Ó Ríordáin, many of his poems struggle with the isolation, guilt and loneliness caused by this dimension of Irish life.

Another modern concern of Ó Ríordáin is 'identity'. Seán Ó Ríordáin was born in Ballyvourney, County Cork on 3 December 1916. His father, a shoemaker, was a native Irish speaker, as were many in the surrounding area. His mother was an English speaker who spoke little Irish. The future poet spoke mostly English at home. All teaching was through Irish in the primary school at Sliabh Riabhach. During the War of Independence and the Civil War, this region of West Cork near the Kerry border was nationalist and Republican. The Revivalist writer An tAthair Peadar Ó Laoghaire was from the locality. Seán Ó Ríordáin was influenced by Ó Laoghaire's autobiography *My Own Story* (1915), which was read to him as a child. He recorded in his journal that ever 'since then every placename mentioned in the book is magic to me'. The district had a very strong tradition of poetry, folklore and storytelling. The conflict of the worlds of English and Irish is articulated directly in 'O Language Half Mine', and the concomitant theme of identity in poems such as 'Footprints' and 'Exchange'. The modern dilemma of identity was obviously heightened by the duality of Ó Ríordáin's upbringing within such a community.

When Seán Ó Ríordáin was eleven, his father died of tuberculosis. In 1932 his family moved to Inniscarra, just outside Cork City. He himself was diagnosed with TB in 1938, and spent the rest of his life in and out of various sanatoria. In accord with the period's medical practice of isolating those suffering from the disease, a room was built for him at the back of the Inniscarra home separating him from the rest of the house, his family and the outside world. A preoccupation with sickness and alienation predominates throughout his work.

He attended secondary school in the North Monastery and was an average student. In 1936, shortly after completing his secondary education, he was given the position of clerk in the motor taxation office of Cork City Hall. He was frequently absent from work because of illness, hospitalised in Mount Desert, near Duhallow in North County Cork, and later in Sarsfield's Court, close to Cork City. He forged a lifelong friendship with the writer and scholar Séamus Ó Coigligh, who also worked in the City Hall. He took early retirement from the City Hall in 1965, and in 1969 was given a part-time position in the Department of Irish under the auspices of Professor R.A. Breatnach at University College Cork. The conditions of this position were that he was to be available to students five hours a week and to give six lectures a year on literary and cultural themes. Ó Ríordáin's influence was seminal on a younger generation of poets and writers in Cork – writing in both Irish and English – during the early 1970s and 1980s.

Seán Ó Ríordáin never married, nor did he have a life-long partner; he lived a withdrawn life as a bachelor. He began to visit the West Kerry Gaeltacht in the 1940s and forged a relationship with that community of Irish speakers. He recognised the strong Gaelic tradition of the south-west of Ireland and breathed new life into it with poems like 'To Daniel Corkery' and 'Return Again'. In the latter poem Ó Ríordáin asks the reader to 'untackle/ the halter of the English Pegasus:/ Shelley, Keats and Shakespeare./ Return again to what is us....' This connecting back with the Gaelic tradition became particularly important to younger poets such as Liam Ó Muirthile, Nuala Ní Dhomhnaill, Michael Davitt, Louis de Paor and Colm Breathnach. Ó Ríordáin's poetry began a renaissance in poetry. His counterpart in Irish music was Seán Ó Riada, who was in the UCC music department around the same time as Ó Ríordáin. Between them they revolutionised Irish poetry and music.

At the same time Seán Ó Ríordáin did not eschew the English tradition. He was immersed in modernist poetry from Eliot onwards, merging modernism with the Irish Gaelic tradition. As Gearóid Denvir states in his entry on Seán Ó Ríordáin in *The Encyclopaedia of Ireland* (2003): 'His first collection, *Eireaball Spideoige* (1952), at once grounded in Irish tradition and thoroughly modernist in sensibility and tone, revolutionized poetry in Irish. The poems, both individually and as an integrated aesthetic statement, seek to answer fundamental questions about the nature of human existence and the place of the individual in a universe without meaning [...] The book was haughtily dismissed by Máire Mhac an tSaoi in two reviews as being merely "the common scruples of conscience of an ordinary Catholic" and, moreover, as being narrated in a discourse that was non-Gaelic. These reviews upset Ó Ríordáin deeply, and he did not publish his second collection, *Brosna*, until 1964.' It is, perhaps, true to say that it is this very marriage of the Gaelic world with the non-Gaelic, with modernism, which is Ó Ríordáin's greatest contribution to writing in Irish and to the Irish dual tradition. He revitalised poetry in Irish with a humanity that innately understood 'We issue from everywhere.'

Seán Ó Ríordáin's publisher was Sáirseál agus Dill in Dublin. His collections of poems after *Eireaball Spideoige* and *Brosna* are *Línte Liombó* (1971) and the posthumous book edited by Seán Ó Coileáin *Tar Éis Mo Bháis* (1978). He received a D. Litt from the National University of Ireland in 1976, the year before he died. A selection of his poems, *Scáthán Véarsaí*, was published in 1981, edited by Cian Ó hÉigeartaigh. In 1964 *Rí na n-Uile* was published – a collection of modern Irish versions of old Irish poems, in collaboration with An tAth Seán Ó Conghaile. Seán Ó Ríordáin wrote a much-read and admired column for *The Irish Times*. He also kept a diary from the late 1930s until his death. This diary is now in the Library at University College Dublin. It is an important literary document which has not been edited or published in its entirety, although extracts from it were published in Seán Ó Coileáin's biography *Seán Ó Ríordáin: Beatha agus Saothar* (1982). The journal gives a background to his poems and to his aesthetic and literary life. The entry for 7 October

1956 indicates how important this diary was to him: 'This life, it seems, is a storm. Look at the features of an old person. It's clear he has gone through dread, through storm, and that he believes he's lucky because he has survived. I'm not quite an old man yet. That leaves me in the eye of the storm. I'm in danger of drowning. A person has many tricks to quieten the roar of the storm – alcohol, women, football, religion, work etc. This book, it appears, is my own escape route. It's no wonder there would be much childishness and tomfoolery in it. It's a drug. It's shelter. It's in full flight.' He wrote the last entry in his journal only days before he died on 21 February 1977. Ó Ríordáin is buried in Reilg Ghobnatan, in his native parish of Ballyvourney, County Cork.

*

Because my Irish is not adequate and since only a handful of poems are to be found in the anthologies, I asked the poet Liam Ó Muirthile to help me understand the poems. Liam Ó Muirthile himself is one of the poets who came out of University College Cork while Seán Ó Ríordáin was present there. He helped me over three or four years. He also sent me samples of the diary, from which the entry quoted above is taken. These translations, which appear in the order in which they were published within the books, would not have been possible without him, and for his help and patience I am grateful. It is a matter of ethical regret that the originals do not appear side by side with these translations. Every effort was made to acquire permission to publish, with these translations, the original poems from Seán Ó Ríordáin's publisher. Out of deference to the originals, and as a reference, I have set each poem's Irish title with the translated title in the title index.

Perhaps the best way to appreciate and understand a

poet in another language is to translate the poetry. My approach to translating the poems of Ó Ríordáin has varied from poem to poem. Of the three types of translation characterised by John Dryden, I have chosen to bypass 'metaphrase', which is a crib – the turning of a poem word by word and line by line prosaically from one language into another. I have mainly worked within Dryden's second category of 'paraphrase' or 'translation with latitude', which allows the translator to keep the author in view while altering words, but not sense, in poems like 'My Mother's Burial' and 'Fever'. In these poems I have attempted to stay true to the sense of the poem, as well as to its rhyme and general prosody, which, of course, is part and parcel of its meaning. I kept Paul Goodman's reflections on translation in mind: 'To translate, one must have a style of one's own, for otherwise the translation will have no rhythm or nuance, which comes from the process of artistically thinking through and molding the sentences; they cannot be reconstituted by piecemeal imitation. The problem of translation is to retreat to a simpler tenor of one's own style and creatively adjust this to one's author.' I have rarely extended my translating into Dryden's third category, 'imitation', which Katharine Washburn, in her introduction to *World Poetry* (1998), describes as 'a translation that departs from the words and sense of the poem where the translator sees fit.' An example is 'Freedom' in which Ó Ríordáin's technique, frequent throughout his poetry, of inventing portmanteau words is co-opted freely.

Generally speaking, what English cannot correspond with is the rhythm and 'local music' of the Irish, which are so powerful in the poems of Seán Ó Ríordáin. David Ferry laments in his own translation of Vergil: 'But the

Latin line, in the authoritative implacable finality of the grammatical structure [...] could not be brought across, and when I read my attempt I feel haunted by its absence.' A similar lament keens in the background of these translations, published so that the world of English speakers in Ireland and outside of Ireland finally gets a sense of the quality and range of the poems of Seán Ó Ríordáin, along with his importance within the Irish literary tradition.

Greg Delanty

Burlington, Vermont
September 2007

from A Robin's Tail

from *Eireaball Spideoige* (1952)

Apologia

Life brimmed over,
every living thing turned to froth,
I churned the cream into butter,
anxious not to waste a drop.

Though I'm no great shakes as a churner
and life is seldom condensed,
there's demand for every grade of butter
throughout the slack season.

The Blind Man in the Studio

'Sit down and I'll sketch you,'
I said to the blind man,
'There's a chair near you there in the corner.'
He turned his head,
stretched out a hand well-versed in searching,
every finger freestroking
like a musician fingering his instrument.
He played the renowned air,
a score of silent notes,
the soft lament of the blind.
He grasped the back of the chair
and eased himself down
on its bank.
He's off now combing his hair;
Ah, my blind rake!

The Cure

The afternoon was all social intercourse,
the sky bled, the blood drained from the clouds,
the manky earth left behind.
I was surrounded by a revelling rabble
mocking and swearing mindlessly.
Back home I couldn't sit still,
courting the learned tomes
with a bloody ache in my soul.
Behind on the hill a fella courts a young one.
   I lowered myself in the usual sordid way,
   the sole handy remedy for pain.

The Question

Death hurries for me in summer.
Will I pluck a flower before its entry?
Or will I quietly tear away at my desire
hoping I'll be plucked into eternity?

Is eternity, as the saints say,
behind the worm and clay of the cemetery?
Is the kiss I'm deprived of today
to be found in the life beyond decay?

Odi Profanum Vulgus

A person isn't an apprentice shoemaker
for long before his behaviour shifts.
From then on he speaks as every maker
down the years who fashioned boots.

It isn't long before a person crafting poetry
separates from the crowd's insanity,
takes the road of ages
with something like a cleric's dignity.

Old Poets, Teach Me Your Call

There are words, if only I knew them,
hidden in the haze of time.
I'm eternally searching for their whereabouts
since the age drove me astray.
They're scattered in scholarly books,
in the memory of old people,
moseying the roads of my own memory.
Oh, I pass them by without a notion.

There's a vision there and I know it,
welling in the womb of my imagination.
A bodiless bright flame like the wind
in search of a suitable body,
a potential child craving life.
I'm a woman who's neither a virgin nor mother.
Old poets, teach me the call,
entice them into my corpus.

Beggars

I look at life around me
– at the theology
mouthed by the priest,
the blather of a bachelor
who wouldn't touch a woman with a barge pole,
and the clacking of a young one
schooled in the shorthand of chastity –
and I'm sure I catch the limp gratuity
of that begging crew
who stretch out a needy hand
without sparing a single thank you.

The Sin

The shilling moon slips into a cloud purse
    slowly, slowly, shyly,
like a swimming swan caresses a lake,
    tenderly caresses the night.

The moon spills from the cloud's purse
    – the seamless soul of the night –
like assonance falling sweetly through verse.
    I shivered at the coldness of the poetry.

A dreadful holler was flung
    like a shot through the night's pane.
I thought I spotted the slivers
    lying underfoot like a foul stain.

I looked again at the manuscript of verse.
    It was prose instead of poetry.
The moon, clouds and sky turned banal
    after that insult to the soul of night.

Darkness

As I lie in bed tonight,
night heavy on my eyes,
I think – without a tear clouding sight,
without anger, without surprise –
of the lights blown out in my life,
every light put out
by unbelievable misfortune
as if by the howling wind.
Strange that I'm the guy
with every hope snuffed.
Odd that only yesterday
I was a hopeful wretch of a boy.
Now darkness steadily shrouds me.
My eyes distinguish nothing.
The wind is no freer
than those with no light to extinguish.

The Storm

A knocking on the door, not a Christian there,
a blind unremitting wind
makes shreds of the night,
the sound of a dress thrashing on the line,
stabbed by sharp needles of hail.
A petrified old woman wails to heaven,
her eyes to the ceiling of the house
while the beating of the rain
drowns out the words in her mouth.
There she goes gripping a candle anxiously,
securing the window latches.
When the light shows on the pane
a host of raindrops appear.
A freezing spike of rain stabs my hand.
I look down with a start;
it's a drop of ink
from my fountain pen.
A drop of rain would be clear.

Rest

Like a bush bent by the wind
  my soul is bowed tonight.
  There's no shelter east or west.
  Thought is a hole in my head
  the wind blows through without rest.

I'll go to the dancehall.
The solid beat of feet
  and the slang of lust
  will drown out thought a little.
  Then I'll know rest.

But every gob yapped fluently
 – except for my dumb face –
  in a language that's completely
  foreign to that alien place
  where I spend my solitary days.

I'll compose a vocabulary,
a mirror of verse tonight,
out of which a sociable face
will confide in me,
  then I'll know peace.

The Old Harp of Ordinary Things

Cluck, cluck, cluck – it dawned on me,
    the hens being beckoned,
that the words cluck, cluck, cluck are a poem
    straight from antiquity.

You can pluck like Orpheus
    on the old harp of ordinary things.
That echo was heard
    in many a head.

There's an ageless solitude in the cat
    nesting without shame,
the chummy cat lustfully
    lounging on the hearth.

I fall back like a child
    on my elfishness
as my legs stiffen dead,
    asleep with pins and needles.

There's lore in that waking,
    in that awful ticklesome tremor,
the pookas of folklore
    as a kid I imagined.

There, I've touched three strings
    on the old harp of ordinary things:
the ordinary hen cluck, a curled cat on a hearth
    and the leg pinned asleep with pins and needles.

To Daniel Corkery

Get up and sing our thanks to him.
He taught us the way.
He woke the doe of poetry
within the wood of the years.

He made a keen ear of his soul.
He was strict on himself,
on anyone else who shaped a verse.
A band of poets landed

with a bang
on the day's outlandish shore:
Eoghan of the tuneful mouth,
Aindrias Mac Craith, Seán Clárach, Aodhgán.

He set a quiet finger on Aodhgán's pulse.
He believed in its pace.
The day brightened on an antique mind,
the mind of our race.

He returned upstairs with them,
this band of poets.
He had the measure of the Munster crowd,
himself and Eoghan Rua.

He lifted the ear of his race from them,
the ear of the spalpeen.
He couldn't tolerate any poem
except one without flaw.

He's at my side listening all the time.
He's like a second conscience.
The vigour of his discipline is in my rhyme.
I'm haunted.

The dusk of the language in Ireland,
night fogfalling softly like a story.
He listened to a cricket in verse,
caught the heart of the race clearly.

My Mother's Burial

June sun in the orchard,
    the silksusurrus of afternoon,
a damn bee droning,
    ululatearing afternoon's gown.

I pored over a tarnished old letter,
    every word-sup swallowed
constricted my breath,
    every piercing word drew a tear.

I remember the very hand that wrote this,
    a hand as familiar as a face,
a hand meek as an old bible,
    a hand that was a balm when sick.

And midsummer fell back into midwinter,
    the orchard became a white graveyard by the river.
In the centre of the dumb whiteness
    the black hole cried out in the snow.

Brightness of a girl on her first communion,
    brightness of the host on a Sunday altar,
brightness of the milksilk ribboning from the breast
    as they buried my mother, brightness of the sod.

My mind was demented struggling
    to grasp the funeral
when out of the white silence a robin flew down
    gently without fear, without confusion

and stayed above the grave as if aware
    of its errand, hid from everybody,
except the body waiting in the coffin.
    I envied their extraordinary intimacy.

The air of paradise descended on the grave.
    The bird had a terrible saintly gaiety.
I was a man excluded from the secret affair,
    distanced from the grave.

Sorrow's fragrance washed my wanton soul.
    Chastity's snow fell on my heart.
Now my heart is cleansed, I'll bury the memory
    of the woman who carried me in her womb.

The gravediggers appeared with shovels
    rigorously spading clay into the grave.
I looked away, a neighbour brushing his trouser knees,
    the worldliness on the priest's face.

June sun in the orchard,
    the silksusurrus of afternoon,
a damn bee droning,
    ululatearing afternoon's gown.

I'm writing little, lame verses.
    I'd like to grab hold of a robin's tail.
I'd like to scatter those knee scrubbers.
    I'd like to make my way, sadly, to the end of day.

The Giants

Pain descending bit by bit,
    pain on pain.
Torment is nothing
    I try to maintain.

Respite will come at dawn,
    the sun rose,
but pain just grows worse.
    Watch out, Jesus!

Pain continues to argue.
    I am the subject.
There's no word in pain's lexicon
    that I'm not its object.

Devouring me, drinking me,
    milking me.
I'm sincerely well mannered to them.
    I'm all humility.

They take the day.
    I am the loser.
The enemy's in my house; patience is best;
    a chance will appear.

Wait, the pain's gone too far.
    I surrender.
My spirit rears with great cheer
    and hoists a cry,

a scream against God,
    challenging him to throw
everything he's got.
    I'm done for now.

Sweetness descending through the air,
    strength descending.
I see the two great ones side by side:
    God and the scream.

Behind the House

Tír na nÓg is behind the house,
   a fantastic, topsy-turvy place;
four-footed characters pace
   about without shirt or shoes,
   without English or Irish.

A cloak grows on each back
   in this hugger-mugger place,
a tongue's spoken behind the house
   no one could understand but Aesop
   and he's in the dust now.

There's hens and chickens;
   a steady, uncouth duck;
a great black dog hounding the land,
   snarling at everyone;
   and a cat milking the sun.

In the far corner there's a rubbish heap;
   all the wonders of the world lie there:
a candlestick; buckles; an old straw hat;
   a mute toy trumpet;
   and a white kettle like a goose.

It's there the tinkers come,
   saintly, harum-scarum,
kin to the back of the house;
   it's here they seek alms
   at the back of every house in Ireland.

I'd like to be behind the house
    in the darkness, late,
to witness, in the moonlight
    the scholarly pooka himself,
    Professor Aesop.

Exchange

'Come here,' said Turnbull. 'Take a look at the sorrow
    in the horse's eyes;
if you'd hooves under you like that, you'd have sorrow
    in your eyes also.'

It was as clear as day he knew the sorrow
    in the horse's eyes,
reflecting so deeply he plunged
    finally into the horse.

I looked at the horse to catch the sorrow
    standing out in his eyes,
and saw Turnbull's eyes gaping straight at me
    out of the horse's skull.

I looked at Turnbull and checked again
    and saw on his cheeks
the tremendous eyes mute with sorrow –
    the horse's eyes.

Mount Melleray

A storm of snoring last night in Melleray,
feverish days of soft habit sink me,
days of lazing on the hot bed of life,
the lice of lust a gorging army.

During the night a whirlwind of footsteps,
the monks striding to mass,
joy a twirling jig in the air,
the monks' soles beating time.

A brother dished up food in the refectory,
a serving of soft silence his balm,
a blessed awkwardness writ all over him,
the natural humility of a good man.

A splash of light poured slowly
through the beehive of a window,
moulding the monk from head to toe.
The sunbeam commenced the reading.

A cold monk took over.
The clock cleared its throat.
The monks of light were quenched,
the Word snuffed out.

The compline hand struck, every guest
trekked sheepishly to the chapel.
The monks were white as snow,
the rest of us dark as hell.

Clammy beads clung to my hand,
my pants stuck tight at the knee,
a cowled procession of monks wound by.
It felt wrong to even sneak a peek,

but I gawked without pity or sympathy,
the way folk long ago must have gaped
at Lazarus as he rose from the dead,
their eyes all agog.

One by one the monks filed down
to the prayerful graveyard,
the cemetery cowled in a fog of down,
a ghostly pallor on afternoon's cheek.

'Death ices life around here.
Death is the only abbot they heed.
The monks are under his thumb.
It's for his sake they fast and abstain.

A mere lad hobbles like a feeble old man.
It's an insult to God.
Such an injustice
clouds the very sun,

lays midnight all over midday
shrouds the river's grace,
plants lust in a dove's mind
and fills the world with shame.

The boy hasn't a bull's notion of the mind
teeming with lively, fecund thoughts.
Never mind the abbot, the clock, the rule.
Lie down with your fantasy.

He'll never quaff the love of a woman
which, like faith, moves mountains,
which once gave Dante a vision of heaven,
angels alighting in verses.'

So spoke the haughty, rebellious ego
blinded by life's fury. But then,
hearing the music over my head, it dawned
that the flock's greater than any one person.

I gazed back on the desert of my life,
the beads sweating in my hands,
sin, sloth and perverse waste,
the terrible, stinging years.

I looked upon the monks' time
and recognised a poem on the spot,
metre, clarity, depth and rhyme.
My mind leaned towards an answer.

Confession was a relief this morning,
a weight was lifted. I was myself.
I vaulted and danced in Latin.
I almost landed on the floor of heaven.

Another time I brimmed with self-confidence,
my veins burst with life.
I imagined the Holy Spirit reigned in my brain,
my words poured from heaven.

But now again my mind is spancelled
to God's church. I'd even call a priest a eunuch.
Faith's all crawthumpery. Let's drink without truck.
We'll live it up until we croak.

Monks drone on like bees in my brain.
My mind's bent by a question
that weighs back and forth.
Compline's suddenly over.

A storm of snoring last night in Melleray.
Maelstrom days of soft habit sink me.
The days to come are withheld in God's fist.
This a drowned man's clutch on a sugawn of poetry.

Death

Death was beside me,
I consented to follow
without delay or tears.
I stared at yours truly
in sheer astonishment
and said:
'So, that's me
entirely.
Well, cheerio
now, laddie.'

Looking back
on the time
death came
pronto to me
and I had
to submit,
I reckon I experienced
the delight of a date
greeting her dandy,
though I'm no lady.

Music

Music impresses the air,
gathers the surrounding space.
walls of music everywhere,
a soundproof roof above me.

Within my cave of music
I read a book of verse,
poetry from Wales.
It shut me out initially.

Life's chitter-chatter tripped up
the heels of harmony,
till suddenly the music cut me free
from the static of the everyday.

A groundswell of music hit me.
I held a book of poems.
I took a tight grip
on the slender verse.

I kissed the woman from Wales,
kissed her mouth to mouth,
music pressed to music,
music spraying through music.

With a slip from Wales
and a slip from my own mind
I built a sound hut
inside the music, an air-hive mound.

An Island and Another Island

I

Before Heading to St Finbarr's Island

There's an English chap fishing on the lake.
The bare truth crowds the island.
I'll comb memory and the stones
and with reverence bathe my hands.

I'll row across and pay attention
to the marrow-thoughts of saints
which Finbarr bequeathed to the island.
I'll hear them in the grey matter of air.

II
Doubt before Starting for the Island

Finbarr, I'm taken with the site of your reflection,
but years of meaningless words
and deafness are like a furry fungus
downing my own reflection.

Buried thoughts
are gathered in a heap
with the edges blunted
in my mind.

Saints and children,
scrape the mildew
from Christ's features
and my reflection.

The air is like a yawn
stretched on my soul.
Is Finbarr in the wind
billowing in me?

Finbarr and the saints
are in the clay many a day.
Confusion hoodwinks me,
gives me a start.

I'm weary at heart
of dull words,
deception or the devil
delude me.

III
The Start

There's a rumour of saints everywhere.
The wind is threading the air.
An ancient prayer slips memory.
My thoughts are blown astray once more.

Here in the pen of saints' reflections
a new image leaps to mind:
the song of a bird
showering scorn on life.

The music the bird pours forth
is his own island world; everyone
is granted an island of their own.
Those who ignore that shore haven't a prayer.

IV
Everyone's Island

In the mind's core
there's an island of serenity.
You head to that shore –
it's your true island.
You're there already.
Don't be scared of yourself
though your very self
burns you alive.
You're cursed truly
by life itself –
you're just chatter
from one mouth to another,
although, originally
you were a bright prayer
on the lips of God.
You turned from your true country
out of lust for life,
but you're still a prayer
on the island of serenity,
still a whisper
on the lips of God
ever since you teasingly danced
on the tip of life.

V

Saint Finbarr's Island

A showery afternoon in Gougane,
fog corroding a cliff.
I looked on the island for a sign,
found it in the trees.

Stunted branches rose about me,
entangled in each other.
They writhed this way and that
like a body burning alive,

or like writing penned on parchment
and crazily scribbled over.
I saw a stumpy snoz, knee, hump, and spawg.
Finally I made out the gait of Gandhi.

O Finbarr, I see in the twisted branches
that the godly man and the worldly man
fought it out there
in your sanctum stumptorum.

When the fog of our flesh lifts
a weird beauty will show in the striae.
Your form will be measured for itself
within the skeleton of light.

The trees exult in their own form,
in the slantwise way they look,
in everything stunted crooked,
abhorring anything soft and upright.

The writing of the trees is masculine.
There's not a breast or curve in any character.
The imprint of the monk is everywhere.
Finbarr is in the loop of every limb.

Everyone's version of God's freedom
is his own island.
Christ flows through each vein.
It's in the turn of everybody's words.

This blueprint of each person's island
is the island home of Finbarr,
Christ flowing through each vein
and the weird gnomeness of limbs.

VI
The Englishman and Myself

There's an English chap fishing on the lake.
He doesn't dwell much on the island.
Maybe his ideal island
is simply angling on the lake.

I'll get up now and head back.
I'll say cheerio to the marrow thoughts of saints.
I'll cover up the truth like everyone else,
return to the chitter-chatter of life.

Freedom

I'll go out and mingle with people.
I'll head down on my own two feet.
I'll walk down tonight.

I'll go down looking for Confinedom,
counteract the rabid freedom
coursing here.

I'll fetter the pack of snarling thoughts
hounding me
in my aloneness.

I'll look for a regular chapel
chockablock with people
at a set time.

I'll seek the company of folk
who never practise freedom,
nor aloneness,

and listen to pennythoughts
exchanged
like something coined.

I'll bear affection for people
without anything original
in their stockthoughts.

I'll stay with them day and night.
I'll be humble
and loyal to their snuffed minds

since I heard them
rising in my mind
without control.

I'll give all my furious affection
to everything that binds them
to every stockthing:

to control, to contracts, to the community temple,
to the poor common word,
to the concise time,

to the cowl, to the cockerel, to the cook,
to the weak comparison,
to the coward,

to the communal mouse, measure and flea,
to the code, to the codex,
to the codicil,

to the cocky coming & going,
to the costly night gambling,
to the conferred blessing,

to the concerned farmer testing
the wind, contemplating
a field of corn,

to co-understanding, to co-memory,
to the co-behaviour of co-people,
to the co-stockthing.

And I condemn now and for ever
the goings-on of freedom,
independence.

The mind is finished
that falls into freedom's abyss.
There's no hills made by God there,
only abstract hills, the range of the imaginary.
Every hill crawls with desires
that climb without ever reaching fulfilment.
There's no limit to freedom
on Mount Fancy,
nor is there limit to desire,
nor any relief
to be found.

Syllabling

A nurse in the infirmary
brightness of afternoon,
pulses in the bed
pounding away time.
She stood at the head
of each man and read,
jotted down rhythm
syllabaaing fingers –
syllabiahing in time
out of the ward
leaving a band
of pulses beat time.
On the other hand the Angelus
syllabelled on trembling lips,
but the amens died down
to a mumble in the ward,
drowned out by the chorus
in the monastery of flesh.
The pulses like monks
celleabaling heavenward.

from Kindling

from **Brosna** (1964)

O Irish In My Pen

O Irish in my pen
have you lost your line?
Are you a poor bastard
without lineage?

Does anyone on your routine
accompany you to the well?
Is there any word from Hippocrene
can ease your parched mumble?

Do you feel pain?
Are you a lovely female?
Are you at your best
whichever way you rest?

Whatever side you lie at night,
whatever way
you stretch your lush limbs
would the bishops, brothers and priests say
it's improper to dwell on your body
for fear of hell?

Do the words belong
to you when I do wrong?
When my heart hides something,
is it you who says nothing?
Do you sense the insane
turmoil in my brain?

I lug you everywhere.
Lady Nemesis bugs my ear.
You suck up to that foreign whore.
I slip thoughts to you
that I pilfer from her.
It's your appearance that lies
    there behind the exchange of eyes.

Footprints

Now I'd like to meet him
when it's out of the question.
He went southwards that morning.
He'll never return.

A sunny morning in Kerry,
the skitting stream can be heard
like hidden girls' giggling in the gully
as I pass that way.

He walked with me that morning,
the pair of us on the one path.
It struck me walking back,
noticing his footprints in the mud,

that he wasn't here till he left.
Being here he can never be there.
That character who's gone
is a complete person.

May the soul of that fellow
who accompanied me,
and the souls of all my diverse selves
who follow, be saved for ever.

Those feet that printed the mud
were also mine, yet
it wasn't I who was the one with him
listening to the stream.

I wasn't born until he died.
There are many 'me's in myself.
I die with every word,
but I rise with every breath.

The new me tags me
until one becomes the other.
Myriads pen these verses,
a new person with every breath.

Layer by layer I peel
these characters from my heart.
It's no wonder I'm fond of the prints
in the mud as I depart.

Claustrophobia

Beside the wine
a candle, terror.
The statue of my Lord
appears without power.
What's left of night
teems into the yard;
the government of night
rules outside my window.
If my candle is snuffed,
later on, in spite of me,
the night will spring
into my lung;
my mind will be overwhelmed;
terror will smother me;
I'll become night;
I'll be a live dark:
   but if my candle holds
   a single night
   I'll be a republic of light
   until day dawns.

The Maneen

This poem does not refer to Ezra Pound, but to a native Irish speaker from Dún Chaoin in County Kerry. He was one of the liveliest and sharpest speakers of Irish in his time. He was not a small man, but to look at him one would think that all his parts were compact because he carried himself with great nobility.

'The maneen is entitled to a house and bit of ground,'
the woman spoke up for Pound.
Pound entered her customised word
and completely settled down.

I didn't see the real Pound till she spoke.
I scanned him from the mound
of the title she set him up on
and to my mind it was wholly sound.

Pound is grounded for good in her word.
Since Pound is a maneen,
his whole frame – from the ground he stands on
to his crown – is in accord with her decree.

Pound is enthroned in her word.
He has peace of mind.
No matter how unsettled our world,
Pound will always hold his ground.

A Week

Monday a wind rising,
Tuesday the air rustling,
Wednesday a branch sobbing,
Thursday ripped through clothing,
Friday kept keening,
Saturday got a wind-hugging,
but on Sunday God's son shushed
the waves and the wind
and the Lord's day was hushed
    since mass-goers crossed the sea from the Blasket.

Frozen

One frosty morning I went out.
A handkerchief hung from a bush.
I reached to put it in my pocket.
Frozen, it slid from my grip.
It wasn't a live cloth slipped my grasp,
but a thing that died last night on a branch.
There I was, wracking my brain
till its correlative dawned on me:
    that time I kissed a relative
    and she stretched in her coffin, petrified.

The Moths

The sound of a fragile moth, a page turning,
the brushing of its winglets
in the bedroom, a night in autumn,
the torment of something frail.

Another night in a dream I felt
a pair of moth wings,
expansive as the wings of an angel,
fragile as a female.

It was my role to handle them
and not let things go amiss,
to take them without harm
and bring them bliss.

But I spilt the blessed powder
finely sprinkled on each wing.
I figured I'd never be numbered
one of the macho men

who strutted straight out of my confusion
bragging, as usual, of their prowess,
scoring each other from one to ten.
Everyone, but myself, was in.

The sound of a fragile moth, a page turning,
the soiling of the moth film,
an autumn night and the moths fluttering.
I dwell too much on their minor commotion.

In Absentia

There's hardly anyone there.
Most are out of it.
Our concern and our care
is not in being there
    but not to feel the being there.

If being there wasn't so dull
why would we need to pass the time?
Why would we drink
except to be always out of it
    and never settle within ourselves?

Whatever else you wait for,
do not wait for your self.
Whatever you see,
don't see yourself above anyone else,
    to be blind to your own self is best.

What is fame or reputation worth?
Who'd be listening to you?
Who'll pass judgement on a poem
if everyone is outside of it
    except for Sweeney the madman?

The whole crew is on the run.
Everyone's running from themselves.
The whole lot are out of it.
Is there anyone, besides a saint, within
    the abandoned hearth of God?

And still if someone says to you
'You'll find it behind the house,'
don't pay the slightest heed.
You'll cop on yourself much quicker.

And still if anyone says to you
'It's in the pile of ramshackle things,'
don't go outside
searching for it all day.

It's neither here nor there.
It's in no particular place.
It is only outside
and it'll stay outside without being found.

Wisdom will only come
like a leaf on a tree.
Then it'll be inside
   and each person will be aware.

The Praise

It was then that everyone asked Dallán Forcaill, the chief poet of Ireland, had he any praise for Colm Cille. Dallán said that he had, and he began to praise Colm Cille: 'Grant me, while you are alive, reward for my praise,' says Dallán. 'I will grant Heaven to everyone who commits this praise to memory,' says Colm Cille.
                    Beatha Cholm Chille, Mánas Ó Domhnaill

Praise God, poet.
If it's sound, then it'll be a passport
into paradise for whomever
learns it by rote.

If you know by heart
the praise that Dallán Forcaill
gave Colm Cille in Ulster,
you'll be granted God's kingdom.

You think that odd, poet,
you reckon it's brazen
to tout heaven to anyone
who'll remember what you wrote.

But get this, poet,
it's not you who snatched the lines mid-air
and set them on fire,
accompanied by an angelic choir.

You just bumped into the thought
strolling through the mind of God
and found yourself there with Him, poet,
unexpectedly, in the same step.

O Language Half Mine

Who tied this bond between us,
O language half mine?
If you won't fully have me, what's the use?
I'm not much good at giving line.

There's another one after me.
She says 'You're mine.'
I'm caught between the pair of you
and am torn in two.

I need to be always around you,
taken solely by you
or else I'll be robbed of your refuge
and robbed of myself.

A half a mind never grinds properly.
I have to give in to you totally,
even though I'm not at home with you entirely,
O language half mine.

Fever

The mountainous climb out of the bed,
its sickly sweltering core
is a long way from the floor.
　　Miles and miles away
　　people still sit and stand.

We're here in the locality of sheets.
We can barely recall a chair.
　　Once we stood sound on level ground,
　　in a time of walking, long ago.
　　We were as tall as the window.

A picture swells off the wall.
The frame melts into a haze.
A lack of faith can't halt it.
　　Things close in around me,
　　the world comes apart.

A locality is forming in the ether,
a neighbourhood perches on my finger.
I could easily pluck off a chapel.
　　There are cows on the road to the north.
　　The cows of eternity are not as quiet.

Silence

I'm a long time silent.
It might be like this to the end of the line.
I can't recall exactly
 – no matter how much I wrack my brain –
where I put the key that stormy night.
My mind is locked shut.
I can't find any way
to Ríordáinise the word-drift
that every odd tide
washes up on the headland.
My mind is adrift.
Take it easy now.
The key's in a safe place.
Maybe there's nothing there anyway.
Don't take a tack
of notice of the sea and all its wrack.
Be content with a silent mind.

Tulyar

Eh Tulyar, ya Stallion,
purchased by de Valera from the Aga Khan,
my country was a great one for the soutane,
a country of virgins, of abbots,
of psalters and gospels
and frugal friars with expansive erudition.
Ah Tulyar, that's history.
But come here, Stal.
Did you not think it queer
that an artist of your prowess, stature and fame,
of your super seed above all other steeds,
should come
to practise his art amongst us
in this isle of saints and scholars,
the isle blessed by Patrick himself?
It's not that your riding is a sin,
but that your coming stirred us up.
It wasn't Patrick's gospel you brought,
but another mentality
that Eisirt would understand.
A sin is much less of a sin, Stal,
since you came in our midst,
an official public stud
functioning on behalf of the state.
    Had we actually become sterile,
    needing you, our exemplary Stal?
    Would we have turned heretical
    unless you were made official?

The Duck

Here's the story of the duck,
a bird eternally stuck
with a gammy gait.
That's her fate,
the epitome of dumb,
sans rhyme or rhythm,
awkwardly wagging about,
propped on a sagging butt.
You'd swear by her plucky way
she was about to hatch a bardic lay
when it's clear to those who know
she's hardly able for vers libre.

Colm

To Colm, son of Seamus Murphy, sculptor

Your teartantrum, Colm, is a drum
    on the gig of this whirligig.
Tears suit your one year.
    You're at it constantly.

Ah, helpless Colm, why such sorrow?
    Tell me, your godfather.
Is smallness the reason,
    not spotting your own likeness?

Though you're still small,
    you'll fill out over the years,
unlike that stiff array
    your father made of stone and clay.

Being small is no shame,
    you can't become a man before time.
Being small of mind is far worse
    than being small in frame.

The Mad Woman

Her distress is kindling since noon.
It'll persist till her mind erupts.
The whole room is a tinder box.
She strikes the answers like matches off herself.
She'll be dispatched to the madhouse at first light;
the room, the answers and herself finally put out.

Dread of the Dead

The room's taut with dread of the dead.
Their fury can't be subdued.
There's no one alive here but myself.
I sense her all around
though she's three months underground.
Every noise I make
has her on the brink
of appearing above ground.
Quiet. Don't let the newly dead,
barely asleep, hear a sound.

The Two Voices

Oh, composer of verses
you're gregarious too.
People hover about you.
You're in the thick of them.
When you talk with people
you converse out of their midst.
You chat, inclined to people,
as they chitchat with you.

Oh, fellow in the thick of people,
you're also a poet.
You're set deep in your people.
You're way beyond them.
When you jaw with people
you don't converse from their midst that much,
nor do your words issue out of them,
but out of yourself, your own church.

Clarity

Last night I went on a drinking spree.
This morning I see the world clearly.
I can't recall a world so spick and span
as this one on the outskirts of our rantan.

There's not a word without clarity,
not a neck's crook, nor a head's pole.
Here bottle is the essence of bottle –
everything becomes whole.

Everything is clear as day,
everyone's story.
For the first time it dawns on me
why it's hunkydory.

Catology

The cat loves her own body.
She adores stretching her limbs.
When she stretched herself tonight,
cats rained in cataracts from her.

She flows from cat to cat,
releasing them with each roll
as if she wasn't a cat, but a wheel
of cats coming and going.

She is her own catechism,
a cathedral full of herself,
stretching her whole body,
categorising herself with pride.

I have seen scores of cats
incatinate tonight.
No, not scores, but millions
still to be catalogued out of her body.

People

You will play the man here,
you'll play the man there.
You're dispersed in guys,
eternally switching disguise
till, out of characters in yourself,
you'll finally play your own self.

Return Again

Leave the mad world behind,
all that's coursing through us this year of our Lord.
Put it out of your mind:
the Pale, the Battle of Kinsale....
And, since the load's heavy
and the road long, untackle
the halter of the English Pegasus:
Shelley, Keats and Shakespeare.
Return again to what is us.
Ease your mind, relax
your mouth haltered in the syntax
that's thwarted your voice.
Make a clean breast of it.
Make peace with your own race,
with your own place.
It's not natural for anyone to ditch their own country.
On a bright afternoon take the cliff road to West Kerry.
On the horizon you'll catch sight
of the Collective Blaskets, the Subjunctive Skelligs,
the ancient school of Irish shoaling from mouths,
   that's your entry,
   Dún Chaoin in the evening light;
   knock and your true self
   will open sesame.

from Limbo Lines

from *Línte Liombó* (1971)

Limbo Lines

Fair play to the striking lines
that I decided to fire.
They originally signed up for hire,
mad to be enlisted in verse.
Those poxed characters
are now in the hellbox.
No place for that rejected lot
in my wordy universe.
How can I be sure they'd not
do a superior job?
Maybe they'd better suit
what I had to say?
I drafted other recruits
and dispatched them
as if these unnoticed characters
were a foul error.
If I stayed with these lines,
the ones I rejected,
which me or anti-me
would show in the mirror?

Brown Eyes

Those are *her* brown eyes
in her son's head.
I met her beauty
in her gaze.

It was a privileged rendezvous
with her mind and body.
With those two eyes on you
a thousand years passed in a wink.

Those blinking eyes of hers
in him undo me.
Since they appear in a man
I can't face her.

I hadn't a bull's notion
those eyes would turn masculine,
those eyes revealed the spirit
of women to me.

What could be more confusing
than this scenario?
How am I to continue the usual
exchange with them now?

She wasn't the first to peer
out of them, nor is her son.
Nor will he be the last
to stare out of them I reckon.

Is that all that's certain:
a scrap living on,
passing from masculine to feminine,
from mother to son?

Local Music

He heard music in the Dún Chaoin talk
not the words, but the air,
flowing through the *blas* of Munster,
the melody a stranger hears;
a local music
inaudible to the speakers;
a music I've never heard,
being too close,
harnessed in its traces.

A music you still hear in Munster,
even in places its gone under.

Quartz Stone

Naked limbs on the beach,
stomachs and legs sprout
from specks of bathing suits,
a fine afternoon in autumn –

The human admitting itself,
hiding nothing but the belly button
and the body's white confession,
a fine afternoon in autumn –

Except for one black child,
glittering like a quartz stone,
brighter than all the white,
a fine afternoon in autumn.

Transformation

In your mind transform
her cat form into a woman
and you'll see
that she'd be a fine pussy
if only you were a tomcat.

After Sending Him to the Doghouse

Quit bothering me, dog,
I had to put you away.
You were my welcome of welcomes,
and still I called a halt to your day.

You're on your own now, dog,
that's if you're still a dog, and not a shade,
there among your executioners
awaiting the point of the needle.

You were always a big-hearted lapdog.
Your sole gift was love.
The crowd you loved betrayed you
and you only a lost mutt.

You had the manners of a house-trained dog
and the meekness of a stray.
Now all that's left of your spontaneous love
is what dogs my distressed heart today.

Form

Everything that comes
goes and comes back again.
Our first glory returns to form

and becomes a mature adult
as it once became a child.
Youth is set to come round again.

When a child is born
he can't do a thing about it.
What's born is what will be born.

We lose sight
of ourselves every now and then,
looking for the inverse character.

In the end
we'll return with nothing,
except the eternal imprint of our first character.

Light

Night fell bit by bit
till everything was naught.
White&black merged to blackness.
Chairs lost their form,
the room disappeared.
Black deleted every shape:
there's a world in the womb of darkness.
I could trace it with my hand.
I'm left only with its memory.
Memory is slow to create it.

I switch on the light. Abracadabra.
The birth of a room.
Chairs leap from blackness.
The shapes of my hands light up.
Light gives birth to the world.

I switch off the light.
My hands, everything of the world
that was visible, is kaput.

When my light is extinguished,
I'll leave behind a world in shape,
but leave it in a state of darkness.

Live Death

That she died a year ago
was writ all over her face,
no longer lit with that attractive glow,
succumbing to a dark place.
She's buried,
alas, alive in her case.

Work

Work suits the sinner.
He needs it as a cover.
Without it he's naked.
What a thought.

Apathy Is Out

There's not a fly, moth, bee,
man, or woman created by God
whose welfare's not our responsibility;
to ignore their predicament
isn't on.
There's not a madman in Gleann na nGealt
we shouldn't sit with
and keep company, since
he's sick in the head
on our behalf.

There's not a place, stream or bush,
however remote; or a flagstone
north, south, east or west
that we shouldn't consider
with affection and empathy.
No matter how far South Africa,
no matter how distant the moon,
they're part of us by right:
there's not a single spot anywhere
we're not a part of. We issue from everywhere.

To My Friends

You make me livid and not without cause;
your conceited expressions,
your authoritative opinions
prop up your little clique,
indicative of the way the strong treat the weak
in the world today,
not to mention for thousands of years.
You hide behind the false doctrine
you proclaim
in truth's name.
In the name of Christ, whom you castrated,
I'll fight you to the end
 – though you're each my friend –
since I hear the high-pitched echo
of your palaver resounding down the corridor
of history,
wreaking havoc,
on the march.

from After My Death

from *Tar Éis mo Bháis* (1978)

Kitten

To conceive words without an object
ain't enough in the West.
Severed words won't do here,
actions are necessary.

I saw a kitten under a stool tonight
framed perfectly.
He fled from the commotion in sheer
terror, the poor thing.

A shaggy kitten foreboding ill,
 — a smashing sight all right —
but fate never takes a rest
here in the West.

In the East a nod would be enough,
the kitten would be enough.
A kitten's not sufficient here,
as Paul explained Jesus to us.

I'll explain the kitten under the stool tonight
to my fellow Westerners:
they suppose a kitten stockstill under a stool
isn't allkitten.

Author

This particular author said
he'd not compose a word until
he was top notch in Irish.

He spent his youth,
middle age, right
to the end of his days
climbing Mount Irish.

Just as he made the top
he copped it.

Clifftop, Dunquin,

August 1970

This locality is saying something. If it could be put in words, then it would be known that this locality was saying something. The sea, the rocks, the grass, everything growing here says this is the way it is. The people say it. They say it when silent. It is what they say whether speaking or silent. Although it is not what they say. It would be a relief to hear it flushed out in words. It would be nothing new to us. It's said so forcefully by this locality that it must be examined from time to time. It is endurance.

Dithering

I met the wind on the way home.
I turned on my heel and went with her.
She switched direction and left me trekking on,
addled, caught between two winds.

Contents with Irish Titles

from **Limbo Lines – Línte Liombó** (1971)

Index of Titles:

Index of First Lines:

Now I'd like to meet him
O Irish in my pen
Oh, composer of verses
One frosty morning I went out.
Pain descending bit by bit,
Praise God, poet.
Quit bothering me, dog,
'Sit down and I'll sketch you,'
That she died a year ago
The afternoon was all social intercourse,
The cat loves her own body.
'The maneen is entitled to a house and bit of ground,'
The mountainous climb out of the bed,
The room's taut with dread of the dead.
The shilling moon slips into a cloud purse
The sound of a fragile moth, a page turning,
There are words, if only I knew them,
There's an English chap fishing on the lake.
There's hardly anyone there.
There's not a fly, moth, bee,
This locality is saying something.
This particular author said
Those are her brown eyes
Tír na nÓg is behind the house,
To conceive words out of an object
Who tied this bond between us,
Work suits the sinner.
You make me livid and not without cause;
You will play the man here,
Your teartantrum, Colm, is a drum